Table of Contents

I0409236

Chapter 1: Introduction

The Quest for Financial Independence

In today's unpredictable world, the quest for financial independence and the dream of retiring gracefully have taken on new significance. For many, the traditional reliance on Social Security no longer guarantees a comfortable and secure retirement. This book is an exploration of an alternative path—an exciting journey that begins with the joys of dividend growth investing and leads to the possibility of retiring gracefully on dividend income, well before the age when most people turn to Social Security.

The Promise of Dividend Growth Investing

Dividend growth investing is more than just a financial strategy; it's a journey of self-discovery, discipline, and financial empowerment. It's about creating wealth, preserving your purchasing power, and ultimately gaining the freedom to retire on your own terms. This book will be your guide, providing a comprehensive understanding of dividend growth investing, its principles, and its numerous advantages.

Embarking on a Path to Graceful Retirement

While Social Security remains a vital safety net, it may not offer the level of financial security and freedom that you aspire to in retirement. Dividend growth investing offers a compelling alternative—a strategy that not only builds wealth over time but also provides a reliable stream of income, enabling you to retire with grace and peace of mind. This book is your roadmap to comprehending, embracing, and excelling in dividend growth investing, ensuring a future marked by financial independence and retirement on your own terms.

Chapter 2: Unpacking Dividend Growth Investing

In the quest for financial independence and graceful retirement, it's crucial to understand the fundamental concepts that underpin dividend growth investing, as well as the historical context and the magnetic appeal of dividend income.

Defining Dividend Growth Investing

At its core, dividend growth investing is a long-term investment strategy that revolves around the acquisition of shares from companies that regularly distribute dividends and, crucially, exhibit a consistent history of increasing those dividends over time. Unlike investment strategies solely focused on capital gains, such as growth investing, dividend growth investing emphasizes the dual benefit of regular income and potential capital appreciation.

The primary components of dividend growth investing include:

1. **Dividend Income:** The primary objective is to secure a steady stream of dividend income from one's investments. This income can supplement other sources of revenue and serve as a financial buffer.

2. **Dividend Growth:** Investors prioritize companies that not only pay dividends but also demonstrate a commitment to increasing those payouts annually. This commitment reflects the company's financial health and stability.

3. **Long-Term Perspective:** Dividend growth investing is a patient, long-term endeavor. Success is measured not in months but in years and decades.

A Brief History of Dividends

Dividends have a rich historical legacy, dating back to the inception of stock markets. They represent a tangible return on investment for shareholders and a key incentive for owning equity in a company. Understanding this historical context provides valuable insight into the enduring allure of dividend income.

Key Moments in the History of Dividends:

1. **Ancient Roots:** The concept of dividends can be traced back to ancient trading practices, where early investors in ventures were rewarded with a share of the profits.

2. **The Birth of Stock Markets:** With the establishment of stock exchanges in the 17th century, dividends became a structured means of distributing profits to shareholders.

3. **Dividends as a Sign of Stability:** During periods of economic turbulence, companies that continued to pay dividends were seen as stable and trustworthy investments.

4. **Dividends in the Modern Era:** Dividends have remained a cornerstone of investment income, and companies that consistently increase dividends have become known as "Dividend Aristocrats."

The Allure of Dividend Income

The appeal of dividend income within the context of dividend growth investing is multifaceted and resonates with investors seeking financial independence and a graceful retirement.

The Allure of Dividend Income:

1. **Income Stability:** Dividend payments from well-established companies are known for their reliability and consistency. This stability provides a dependable income stream, regardless of market fluctuations.

2. **Intrinsic Value:** Dividends reflect a company's ability to generate profits and share them with shareholders. As such, they represent a tangible return on investment.

3. **The Power of Compounding:** Reinvesting dividends allows investors to harness the magic of compounding. Over time, reinvested dividends can significantly enhance the size of an investment portfolio and the income it generates.

4. **Mitigating Market Volatility:** In times of market turbulence, the steady stream of dividend income can serve as a buffer, reducing the emotional impact of market downturns.

5. **Protection Against Inflation:** Dividend growth stocks often outpace inflation, helping investors maintain their purchasing power over time.

The allure of dividend income is not merely financial; it is also psychological. It offers a sense of financial security, empowerment, and the ability to pursue one's aspirations in retirement with confidence.

As you delve deeper into the world of dividend growth investing, keep in mind that it is not just a financial strategy; it is a journey marked by the promise of financial independence, the wisdom of history, and the undeniable allure of dividend income. In the chapters ahead, we will explore how to put these principles into practice and embark on a path to secure your financial future.

Chapter 3: The Perks of Dividend Growth Investing

In the realm of dividend growth investing, the pursuit of financial independence and graceful retirement is underpinned by three critical pillars: the assurance of steady income, the compounding returns that amplify wealth, and the protection against the eroding effects of inflation.

Steady Income in an Uncertain World

In an increasingly unpredictable world marked by economic fluctuations, geopolitical tensions, and unexpected crises, the concept of a steady income stream holds immense appeal. Dividend growth investing excels in providing this financial stability.

The Pillars of Steady Income:

1. **Reliable Dividend Payments:** Companies with a history of consistent dividend payments are often considered more stable and resilient in the face of economic challenges. This predictability allows investors to rely on dividends as a consistent income source.

2. **Diverse Portfolio Resilience:** By diversifying their investments across various dividend-paying stocks, investors reduce their exposure to the performance of a single company or industry. This diversification minimizes the risk of income disruption due to isolated economic or sector-specific issues.

3. **Lower Dependency on Employment Income:** A reliable dividend income stream reduces reliance on traditional employment income, providing financial flexibility and peace of mind, particularly during economic downturns or job transitions.

The Magic of Compounding Returns

One of the most captivating aspects of dividend growth investing is the magic of compounding returns. This phenomenon, often described as the "eighth wonder of the world" by Albert Einstein, magnifies the growth of wealth over time through the reinvestment of dividends.

Key Elements of Compounding Returns:

1. **Continuous Reinvestment:** As dividend income is received, prudent investors reinvest these earnings back into their investment portfolio, often purchasing additional shares of the same dividend-paying stocks.

2. **Exponential Growth:** Over the years, the reinvestment of dividends results in the compounding effect. The principal investment grows, generating larger dividend payments in subsequent periods.

3. **Accelerating Wealth Accumulation:** Compounding accelerates the rate at which wealth accumulates. This not only enhances the overall size of the investment portfolio but also increases the income generated by the portfolio.

Shielding Against Inflation's Erosion

Inflation, the steady rise in prices over time, can erode the purchasing power of money. For retirees, protecting against inflation's erosion is paramount to ensure that their income retains its real value.

How Dividend Growth Investing Acts as an Inflation Hedge:

1. **Increasing Dividend Payouts:** Companies that consistently raise their dividend payments tend to outpace inflation. As a result, the income received by dividend growth investors grows over time, helping to maintain their purchasing power.

2. **Real Returns:** Dividend income is considered a "real return" because it provides a tangible income stream that has the potential to outpace the rate of inflation. This is in contrast to fixed income investments, which may struggle to keep pace with rising prices.

3. **A Lifelong Hedge:** The protection against inflation provided by dividend growth investing extends throughout an investor's lifetime, making it an ideal strategy for retirees who are concerned about the long-term impact of rising prices.

In a world where financial stability and income security are paramount, the combination of steady income, compounding returns, and protection against inflation's erosion makes dividend growth investing a compelling choice. This chapter underscores the significance of these pillars within the context of dividend growth investing, highlighting how they contribute to the ultimate goal of financial independence and a graceful retirement. As you delve deeper into the world of dividend growth investing, remember that these principles are not only sound but also timeless, offering a solid foundation for building wealth and securing your financial future.

Chapter 4: Setting the Stage for Success

To embark on the path to financial independence and a graceful retirement through dividend growth investing, one must meticulously plan their journey. This chapter explores the crucial steps involved in charting financial goals, constructing a diverse investment portfolio, and mastering the art of research and due diligence.

Charting Your Financial Goals

1. **Clarity is Key:** The first step on this journey is to define your financial goals. Ask yourself: What do you want to achieve with your investments? Your goals may include building an emergency fund, purchasing a home, funding a child's education, or securing a comfortable retirement. Be specific, measurable, and realistic in your goal-setting.

2. **Time Horizon:** Consider the time frame within which you aim to achieve these goals. Short-term goals, such as an emergency fund, may have a different investment approach than long-term goals like retirement.

3. **Risk Tolerance:** Assess your risk tolerance, which is your willingness and ability to withstand fluctuations in your investments. Your risk tolerance should align with your financial goals. For instance, retirement savings may allow for a more moderate risk approach compared to shorter-term goals.

Constructing a Diverse Investment Portfolio

1. **The Power of Diversification:** Diversification is the cornerstone of a resilient investment portfolio. It involves spreading your investments across different asset classes, industries, and geographic regions to mitigate risk.

2. **Asset Allocation:** Determine the appropriate allocation of assets within your portfolio. This allocation should be tailored to your risk tolerance and financial goals. Common asset classes include stocks, bonds, and cash equivalents.

3. **Sector and Industry Diversification:** Within the stock portion of your portfolio, diversify further by selecting dividend growth stocks from various sectors and industries. This approach reduces the impact of poor performance in any single sector on your overall portfolio.

4. **International Exposure:** Consider including international dividend growth stocks to benefit from global economic growth and diversify against country-specific risks.

The Art of Research and Due Diligence

1. **Know What You Invest In:** Before investing in any stock, thoroughly research the company. This includes reviewing financial statements, understanding its business model, and assessing its competitive position within the industry.

2. **Dividend History:** Investigate the company's dividend history. Look for a consistent track record of increasing dividends over time. Companies that have raised dividends annually for many years are often referred to as "Dividend Aristocrats."

3. **Earnings Growth:** Assess the company's ability to generate earnings and cash flow. Sustainable dividend growth is typically supported by strong financial performance.

4. **Valuation:** Evaluate whether the stock is trading at a reasonable valuation. Comparing a stock's current price to its historical price-to-earnings (P/E) ratio can provide insights into its relative value.

5. **Dividend Payout Ratio:** Determine the dividend payout ratio, which is the proportion of earnings paid out as dividends. A lower payout ratio indicates that the company has room to continue increasing dividends.

6. **Management Quality:** Consider the competence and integrity of the company's management team. Look for evidence of shareholder-friendly policies, such as a commitment to returning value to investors through dividends and share buybacks.

7. **Peer Comparison:** Compare the company to its industry peers. How does it stack up in terms of financial performance and dividend growth?

Mastering the art of research and due diligence is essential for making informed investment decisions within dividend growth investing. It ensures that your investments align with your financial goals, risk tolerance, and the principles of this strategy.

In the chapters that follow, we will delve into specific strategies for identifying dividend growth stocks, as well as techniques for effectively managing and growing your dividend portfolio. By carefully charting your financial goals, constructing a diversified investment portfolio, and conducting diligent research, you lay the foundation for a successful journey towards financial independence and graceful retirement.

Chapter 5: Strategies for Success

As you venture deeper into the world of dividend growth investing, you'll discover valuable strategies and tools that can enhance your journey toward financial independence and a graceful retirement. In this chapter, we'll explore three key elements that can significantly impact your success: the Dividend Aristocrats, Dividend Reinvestment Plans (DRIPs), and the power of Dollar-Cost Averaging.

The Dividend Aristocrats: Your Trusted Allies

1. **Defining the Dividend Aristocrats:** The term "Dividend Aristocrats" refers to a select group of companies renowned for their exceptional commitment to increasing dividends annually. To earn this esteemed title, a company must have a history of raising dividends for at least 25 consecutive years.

2. **Why They Matter:** Dividend Aristocrats are like the rock stars of the dividend growth investing world. They possess a track record of unwavering commitment to shareholders and consistent financial performance, making them reliable sources of growing dividend income.

3. **Benefits of Investing in Dividend Aristocrats:** When you invest in Dividend Aristocrats, you are aligning your portfolio with companies that have weathered various economic climates. These companies tend to exhibit resilience during market downturns and consistently provide shareholders with income that outpaces inflation.

Dividend Reinvestment Plans (DRIPs): A Game Changer

1. **Understanding DRIPs:** A Dividend Reinvestment Plan (DRIP) is an investment program offered by many companies that allows shareholders to automatically reinvest their dividend income to

purchase additional shares of the same stock. This reinvestment occurs without incurring brokerage fees.

2. **The Power of Compounding:** DRIPs are a game changer because they harness the magic of compounding. Instead of receiving cash dividends, your earnings are reinvested to acquire more shares. Over time, this can significantly accelerate the growth of your investment portfolio.

3. **A Long-Term Wealth Building Tool:** DRIPs are particularly effective for long-term investors who aim to maximize the compounding effect. They offer a simple and convenient way to build wealth gradually through the reinvestment of dividends.

Dollar-Cost Averaging: Riding Out Market Volatility

1. **The Dollar-Cost Averaging Strategy:** Dollar-Cost Averaging (DCA) is an investment strategy in which you invest a fixed amount of money at regular intervals, regardless of market conditions. This approach allows you to buy more shares when prices are low and fewer shares when prices are high.

2. **Mitigating Market Volatility:** DCA helps mitigate the impact of market volatility and emotional decision-making. By investing consistently over time, you avoid the temptation to time the market, which can be fraught with uncertainty and risk.

3. **Long-Term Success:** DCA is especially valuable for dividend growth investors with long-term goals. It allows you to accumulate shares steadily, benefiting from both dividend income and potential capital appreciation over time.

Incorporating the Dividend Aristocrats into your portfolio, leveraging the power of DRIPs, and implementing a Dollar-Cost Averaging strategy can significantly enhance your dividend growth investing journey. These strategies provide a robust framework for building wealth, compounding returns, and navigating the often-volatile landscape of the stock market. As you progress on this path to financial independence and retirement, remember that patience and consistency are your allies, and these tools are your trusted companions in the pursuit of your financial dreams.

Chapter 6: The Path to Retirement

In the realm of dividend growth investing, the key to achieving financial independence and graceful retirement lies in embracing patience, maintaining a long-term perspective, harnessing the power of reinvestment, and mastering the art of portfolio monitoring and adjustments. This chapter explores the profound significance of these principles in your journey toward financial success.

Patience and the Long-Term Perspective

1. **The Virtue of Patience:** Patience is an enduring virtue that serves as a bedrock of dividend growth investing. It involves the ability to remain steadfast and disciplined in the face of market fluctuations, economic turbulence, and the ebb and flow of stock prices.

2. **Long-Term Commitment:** Dividend growth investors understand that meaningful wealth accumulation and the full benefits of compounding take time. They embrace a long-term perspective that extends beyond months and years into decades. This commitment sets them apart from speculators and short-term traders.

3. **Riding Out Market Volatility:** Patience enables investors to ride out market volatility with resilience. Instead of reacting emotionally to short-term market swings, they remain focused on their ultimate financial goals, knowing that over the long haul, prudent investing prevails.

4. **Compounding Gains:** The true magic of dividend growth investing reveals itself over time. As dividends are reinvested and shares accumulate, the power of compounding is unleashed, leading to exponential portfolio growth.

Reinvestment and the Power of Compounding

1. **The Strategy of Reinvestment:** Reinvestment is the act of channeling your dividend income back into your investment portfolio, often used to purchase additional shares of dividend-paying stocks.

2. **Compounding Returns:** Compounding is the financial phenomenon where the returns generated by an investment are reinvested to generate further returns. This compounding effect magnifies your wealth over time.

3. **Accelerated Growth:** The power of compounding is akin to a snowball rolling downhill. Initially, it starts small, but as it accumulates more snow (or returns), it grows at an accelerating pace. Reinvested dividends have a similar effect on your investment portfolio.

4. **Long-Term Wealth Building:** Reinvestment is a potent tool for long-term wealth building. It ensures that your dividends are not just a source of income but also a force for expanding your investment principal.

The Art of Portfolio Monitoring and Adjustments

1. **Ongoing Vigilance:** Successful dividend growth investing involves more than just the initial selection of dividend-paying stocks. It requires ongoing vigilance to ensure that your portfolio aligns with your financial goals and adapts to changing market conditions.

2. **Regular Review:** Periodically review your portfolio to assess its performance, diversification, and alignment with your objectives. Are your investments still in line with your long-term vision?

3. **Evaluating Dividend Sustainability:** Keep a watchful eye on the financial health of the companies in your portfolio. Are they still capable of sustaining and growing their dividends?

4. **Adjustments When Necessary:** Be prepared to adjust when circumstances warrant it. This could involve rebalancing your portfolio, trimming underperforming stocks, or adding new positions to maintain diversification.

5. **Staying Informed:** Stay informed about economic trends, industry developments, and changes in the market landscape. This knowledge will inform your decisions and help you adapt to evolving conditions.

Embracing patience, maintaining a long-term perspective, harnessing the power of reinvestment, and mastering the art of portfolio monitoring and adjustments are the cornerstones of success in dividend growth investing. These principles not only foster wealth accumulation but also provide the financial stability and flexibility necessary for achieving financial independence and a retirement characterized by grace and security. As you continue your journey, remember that while the path may require dedication and diligence, the rewards are well worth the effort.

Chapter 7: The Turning Point: When Dividends Blossom

In the realm of dividend growth investing, there comes a transformative moment—a financial awakening—that propels investors toward the realization of their retirement dreams. This chapter explores the significance of this moment, the steps involved in paving the way for retirement, and the ultimate liberation that comes with achieving financial independence.

A Moment of Financial Awakening

1. **The Turning Point:** A moment of financial awakening is the point in your journey when you realize that your dividend growth investments have reached a critical threshold. Your dividend income has grown to a level that can meaningfully support your lifestyle or even cover your basic expenses.

2. **Recognition of Possibilities:** This moment is marked by the recognition of new possibilities. You begin to see retirement on the horizon, no longer as a distant aspiration but as a tangible goal that can be achieved.

3. **Financial Empowerment:** The awakening brings a sense of financial empowerment. You realize that you have the means to shape your retirement on your own terms, free from the constraints of traditional retirement age or dependence on government programs.

Paving the Way for Retirement

1. **Assessing Your Needs:** The first step in paving the way for retirement is to assess your financial needs. What kind of lifestyle do you envision in retirement? What expenses will you need to cover, including healthcare, housing, and leisure activities?

2. **Creating a Retirement Plan:** Develop a comprehensive retirement plan that outlines your financial goals, investment strategies, and retirement timeline. Consider consulting a financial advisor to ensure that your plan aligns with your objectives.

3. **Withdrawal Strategy:** Determine your retirement withdrawal strategy. This involves deciding how much of your dividend income you will use for living expenses and how much you will reinvest to maintain and grow your portfolio.

4. **Legacy and Philanthropy:** Consider your desires for legacy planning and philanthropy. How would you like to leave a financial legacy for your heirs or contribute to causes that matter to you?

The Liberation of Financial Independence

1. **Defining Financial Independence:** Financial independence is the point at which your income from dividends, combined with any other sources of passive income, exceeds your living expenses. At this juncture, you are free from the need for traditional employment or government assistance to support your lifestyle.

2. **Liberation and Choices:** Achieving financial independence liberates you to make choices based on your aspirations rather than financial constraints. You can retire when you choose, pursue passions, travel, or dedicate time to interests and causes close to your heart.

3. **Reduced Financial Stress:** Financial independence reduces or eliminates financial stress. You no longer need to worry about job security, economic downturns, or market volatility affecting your livelihood.

4. **Peace of Mind:** The freedom and peace of mind that come with financial independence are immeasurable. It allows you to enjoy your retirement years with confidence and the knowledge that you have secured your financial future.

5. **Passing Down Wisdom:** Achieving financial independence also carries the potential to pass down valuable financial wisdom to future generations. You can impart the importance of responsible financial management and investing to your heirs.

The journey toward financial independence and retirement is marked by a moment of awakening, a pivotal recognition of the possibilities that lie ahead. By carefully paving the way for retirement through thoughtful planning and financial discipline, you can liberate yourself from financial constraints and embrace the freedom to live life on your own terms. This chapter underscores the profound significance of these achievements and sets the stage for the chapters to follow, which will explore legacy planning, retirement strategies, and the joys of pursuing passions in retirement.

Chapter 8: Navigating Retirement with Dividend Income

As you approach retirement, the importance of designing a thoughtful withdrawal strategy, understanding how to navigate market volatility, and embracing the joy of pursuing passions in retirement cannot be overstated. This chapter explores these critical aspects of your journey toward financial independence and a fulfilling retirement.

Designing Your Retirement Withdrawal Strategy

1. **The Fundamentals:** A well-structured retirement withdrawal strategy is essential to ensure that your dividend income supports your desired lifestyle throughout retirement. This strategy

involves deciding how much of your dividend income to use for living expenses and how much to reinvest.

2. **The 4% Rule:** One popular guideline for determining a sustainable withdrawal rate is the "4% rule." This rule suggests withdrawing 4% of your portfolio's initial value in the first year of retirement and adjusting subsequent withdrawals for inflation. It provides a balance between maintaining your purchasing power and minimizing the risk of running out of money.

3. **Flexibility:** Flexibility is key to a successful withdrawal strategy. Be prepared to adjust your withdrawals based on changes in your financial circumstances, market conditions, and unexpected expenses.

4. **Tax Efficiency:** Consider the tax implications of your withdrawal strategy. Depending on your accounts (e.g., taxable, tax-deferred, tax-free), you may want to strategically withdraw from different sources to minimize your tax liability.

Weathering the Storms: Market Volatility and You

1. **The Reality of Market Volatility:** Market volatility is an inevitable part of investing. During retirement, it can be particularly worrying because withdrawals may coincide with market downturns.

2. **Maintaining a Long-Term Perspective:** While market volatility can be unsettling, it's crucial to maintain a long-term perspective. Dividend growth investing aligns with this perspective, as dividend income tends to be stable even when stock prices fluctuate.

3. **Diversification and Risk Management:** Diversifying your portfolio across different asset classes and industries can help mitigate the impact of market volatility. Additionally, having a cash reserve for living expenses can reduce the need to sell investments during market downturns.

4. **Seeking Professional Guidance:** Consider consulting a financial advisor who specializes in retirement planning. They can help you develop a strategy to navigate market volatility and make informed decisions.

The Joy of Pursuing Passions in Retirement

1. **Rediscovering Passions:** Retirement offers a unique opportunity to rediscover and pursue your passions. Whether it's travel, art, music, volunteering, or any other interest, retirement allows you the time and freedom to indulge in what brings you joy.

2. **Living with Purpose:** Engaging in activities you are passionate about can provide a sense of purpose and fulfillment in retirement. Many retirees find that pursuing their passions brings them a new sense of meaning and satisfaction.

3. **Balancing Leisure and Finance:** While it's essential to enjoy your passions, it's also crucial to maintain financial discipline. Your retirement withdrawal strategy should support both your living expenses and the pursuit of your passions.

4. **Legacy and Philanthropy:** Retirement can be an ideal time to consider your legacy and philanthropic goals. You may choose to leave a financial legacy for your heirs or contribute to causes you care deeply about.

Embracing retirement with a well-designed withdrawal strategy, resilience in the face of market volatility, and a commitment to pursuing your passions is the culmination of your journey toward financial independence. It allows you to transition into retirement with confidence, knowing that you have not only secured your financial future but also unlocked the freedom to live life on your terms. In the chapters that follow, we will delve deeper into legacy planning, philanthropy, and the myriad possibilities that await you in retirement.

Chapter 9: Beating the Social Security Clock

As you journey towards financial independence and a fulfilling retirement through dividend growth investing, it's essential to understand the Social Security landscape, strive to achieve retirement ahead of the masses, and consider securing a legacy for future generations. This chapter delves into these critical aspects of your financial journey.

Understanding the Social Security Landscape

1. **Social Security Basics:** Social Security is a federal program designed to provide financial support to retirees, disabled individuals, and survivors of deceased workers. Benefits are based on an individual's earnings history and the age at which they choose to begin receiving benefits.

2. **Supplementing Retirement Income:** While Social Security can be a valuable source of retirement income, it may not be sufficient to cover all your expenses. Dividend growth investing allows you to supplement your Social Security benefits with a reliable stream of income.

3. **Benefits Eligibility:** The age at which you can begin receiving full Social Security benefits is referred to as "full retirement age" (FRA). It varies depending on your birth year, with FRA typically ranging from 65 to 67. You can choose to start receiving reduced benefits as early as age 62 or delay benefits until age 70 for increased monthly payments.

4. **Understanding Spousal Benefits:** Married individuals may be eligible for spousal benefits, which can provide additional income in retirement. Understanding the rules and strategies for spousal benefits can maximize your household's Social Security income.

Achieving Retirement Ahead of the Masses

1. **Early Retirement Through Dividend Growth:** Dividend growth investing offers a path to achieve retirement ahead of the traditional retirement age. By diligently building a portfolio of dividend-paying stocks and reinvesting dividends, you can accelerate your journey to financial independence.

2. **The Power of Consistency:** Consistent contributions to your investment portfolio and the power of compounding returns are key factors in achieving early retirement. Dividend growth investing encourages discipline and a long-term perspective.

3. **Financial Flexibility:** Early retirement provides financial flexibility, allowing you to pursue passions, travel, or engage in philanthropy while you are still active and in good health.

Securing a Legacy for Future Generations

1. **Legacy Planning:** Legacy planning involves considering how you will pass down your assets to heirs and loved ones. It's an integral part of comprehensive retirement and financial planning.

2. **Estate Planning:** Estate planning includes creating a will, establishing trusts, and designating beneficiaries for your assets. These measures help ensure that your assets are distributed according to your wishes.

3. **Philanthropy:** Many retirees choose to leave a legacy through philanthropy. Establishing charitable foundations or donating to causes you care about can have a lasting impact on your community and future generations.

4. **Teaching Financial Wisdom:** Part of securing a legacy for future generations involves teaching your heirs about financial responsibility and investment strategies. Sharing your knowledge and values can empower them to make sound financial decisions.

5. **Tax Considerations:** Consult with financial advisors and tax professionals to optimize your legacy plan and minimize tax implications for your heirs.

Understanding the Social Security landscape, striving for early retirement through dividend growth investing, and securing a legacy for future generations are integral components of your financial journey. By carefully navigating these aspects, you can achieve financial independence, enjoy a fulfilling retirement, and leave a lasting impact on the lives of your loved ones and the causes you hold dear. In the chapters to come, we will explore further strategies for legacy planning and the joys of pursuing your passions in retirement.

Chapter 10: Case Studies in Dividend Dreams

In your pursuit of financial independence and a graceful retirement through dividend growth investing, real-life stories of fellow investors can offer valuable insights. This chapter presents stories of dividend growth investors, lessons from successful retirees, and the strategies they employed to confront challenges and savor their triumphs.

Stories of Dividend Growth Investors

Lisa's Journey to Financial Freedom:

Lisa, a diligent saver, and investor, embarked on her dividend growth journey early in her career. She consistently invested a portion of her income into dividend-paying stocks, often reinvesting her dividends. Over the years, her portfolio steadily grew, and by the time she reached her mid-50s, she had amassed a substantial nest egg.

Key Lesson: Start early, stay consistent, and have a long-term perspective. Lisa's story demonstrates the power of compounding and discipline in building wealth.

David's Early Retirement Dream:

David had a dream of retiring early to pursue his passion for travel and photography. Through dividend growth investing, he meticulously built a portfolio that generated enough income to cover his living expenses. By the age of 45, he had achieved his goal and embarked on a life of adventure.

Key Lesson: Define your retirement goals and tailor your investment strategy to achieve them. David's story showcases the freedom that early retirement can provide.

Lessons from Successful Retirees

Marie's Philanthropic Legacy:

Marie, a retired teacher, had a deep commitment to education. In retirement, she established a scholarship fund for underprivileged students using the dividends from her dividend growth portfolio. Her legacy continues to transform lives and provide educational opportunities.

Key Lesson: Retirement is an opportunity to leave a lasting impact through philanthropy and legacy planning.

John and Mary's Financial Freedom:

John and Mary, a retired couple, relied on their dividend income to maintain their desired lifestyle. Through careful portfolio management and diversification, they weathered market downturns without the need to significantly reduce their withdrawals.

Key Lesson: A well-structured portfolio and withdrawal strategy can provide financial stability during retirement.

Confronting Challenges and Savoring Triumphs

Challenges in Market Turbulence:

All the investors faced challenges during market downturns and economic crises. However, their commitment to a long-term perspective and prudent strategies allowed them to weather these storms and continue their journey.

Key Lesson: Market volatility is part of investing, but a well-thought-out investment strategy and the fortitude to stay the course can lead to eventual triumph.

Savoring the Triumphs:

Each of these investors celebrated their triumphs in different ways—whether through early retirement, philanthropy, or simply the freedom to pursue their passions. They found fulfillment in their financial achievements and embraced the opportunities that their dividend growth portfolios provided.

Key Lesson: The joy of financial independence lies in savoring the fruits of your labor and the freedom it affords.

These stories of dividend growth investors and lessons from successful retirees demonstrate that achieving financial independence and a fulfilling retirement is not an abstract concept; it's attainable through discipline, patience, and prudent investing. As you reflect on these stories, consider how you can apply the lessons learned to your own journey. In the chapters ahead, we will explore legacy planning, philanthropy, and the joys of pursuing passions in retirement, providing you with additional tools and inspiration to realize your financial dreams.

Chapter 11: Strategies for Legacy Planning

As you approach the zenith of your financial journey through dividend growth investing, it's time to contemplate the legacy you will leave behind. This chapter delves into the importance of passing down both wealth and wisdom, ensuring a financially secure future for your heirs, and the profound impact of philanthropy in leaving a lasting mark on the world.

Passing Down Wealth and Wisdom

1. **Financial Education:** One of the most valuable gifts you can bestow upon your heirs is financial education. Sharing your knowledge about investing, saving, and responsible financial management equips them with the tools to navigate their financial futures.

2. **Teaching Values:** Beyond financial knowledge, imparting your values and principles surrounding money is equally vital. Instilling a sense of responsibility, discipline, and stewardship can guide your heirs toward making wise financial choices and decisions.

3. **Open Communication:** Fostering open communication about wealth and financial matters within your family ensures that your heirs are well-prepared to manage any financial inheritance they receive. Encourage discussions about financial goals, investments, and the responsibilities that come with wealth.

Ensuring a Financially Secure Future for Heirs

1. **Estate Planning:** A well-structured estate plan is paramount to ensure that your wealth is distributed according to your wishes. Collaborate with professionals, such as estate attorneys and financial advisors, to create a comprehensive plan that includes wills, trusts, and beneficiary designations.

2. **Asset Protection:** Consider the protection of your assets and wealth. Some heirs may lack financial experience or be susceptible to external threats. Implement asset protection measures to safeguard their inheritance.

3. **Tax-Efficient Strategies:** Explore tax-efficient strategies to minimize the tax burden on your heirs. Effective tax planning can ensure that your wealth is preserved and transferred as efficiently as possible.

Philanthropy and Leaving Your Mark

1. **Philanthropic Goals:** Many retirees find profound fulfillment in philanthropy. Establishing charitable foundations or contributing to causes you are passionate about allows you to make a lasting impact on society.

2. **Legacy of Giving:** A legacy of giving transcends generations. By involving your heirs in philanthropic endeavors, you can instill a sense of responsibility for giving back to the community and carrying forward your philanthropic legacy.

3. **Philanthropy During Your Lifetime:** Consider engaging in philanthropic activities during your lifetime to witness the impact of your contributions firsthand. This can be immensely rewarding and inspiring.

4. **Donor-Advised Funds:** Donor-advised funds offer a structured way to manage and distribute your charitable contributions. They provide flexibility and allow you to strategically allocate funds to causes you support.

Leaving a legacy encompasses more than just the transfer of financial assets; it involves the transmission of wisdom, values, and a commitment to making a positive impact on future generations and society at large. By planning thoughtfully and incorporating philanthropy into your legacy, you can ensure that your wealth continues to serve a meaningful purpose long after your lifetime.

In the upcoming chapters, we will delve deeper into the practical aspects of legacy planning, including the use of trusts, donor-advised funds, and other vehicles to support your philanthropic endeavors while securing a legacy that reflects your values and vision.

Chapter 12: The Future of Dividend Growth Investing

In the realm of dividend growth investing, adaptability is the key to navigating the ever-changing financial landscape successfully. This chapter explores the necessity of adaptation, highlights innovations and opportunities within dividend growth investing, and provides insights on how to stay ahead in a dynamic market.

Adapting to an Ever-Changing Financial Landscape

1. **Economic Cycles:** The financial landscape is subject to economic cycles, including periods of expansion, recession, and recovery. As an investor, understanding these cycles and adjusting your investment strategy accordingly is essential.

2. **Market Trends:** Financial markets are influenced by various trends, including technological advancements, regulatory changes, and geopolitical events. Staying informed about market trends can help you make informed investment decisions.

3. **Changing Investor Preferences:** Investor preferences can shift over time. For example, sustainable investing and Environmental, Social, and Governance (ESG) considerations have

gained prominence. Adapting to these preferences may involve incorporating ESG criteria into your investment choices.

Innovations and Opportunities in Dividend Growth

1. **Technology and Research:** Advances in technology have transformed the way investors research and manage their portfolios. Utilize online tools, data analytics, and research platforms to stay informed about potential dividend growth opportunities.

2. **Global Investing:** The world has become increasingly interconnected, offering opportunities to invest in international dividend-paying stocks. Diversifying your portfolio across global markets can provide access to a broader range of opportunities.

3. **Sector Rotation:** Economic conditions can impact various sectors differently. Consider rotating your investments into sectors poised for growth during specific economic environments. For instance, defensive sectors like utilities may perform well during economic downturns.

4. **Dividend Growth ETFs:** Exchange-Traded Funds (ETFs) focused on dividend growth have gained popularity. These funds offer diversification across multiple dividend-paying stocks and can be a convenient way to access dividend growth strategies.

Staying Ahead in a Dynamic Market

1. **Continuous Learning:** The financial markets are a continuous learning experience. Stay updated on investment strategies, market developments, and financial news. Books, courses, webinars, and seminars can be valuable sources of knowledge.

2. **Diversification:** Maintain a diversified portfolio to spread risk across different asset classes and industries. Diversification can help you weather market volatility and capitalize on opportunities as they arise.

3. **Active Portfolio Management:** Regularly review your investment portfolio to ensure it aligns with your financial goals. Consider rebalancing when necessary to maintain your desired asset allocation.

4. **Risk Management:** Be mindful of risk management. Consider using stop-loss orders to limit potential losses in volatile markets. Having an emergency fund can also provide a safety net during unexpected financial challenges.

5. **Long-Term Perspective:** Dividend growth investing is fundamentally a long-term strategy. Stay committed to your investment goals and avoid being swayed by short-term market fluctuations.

6. **Professional Guidance:** Consult with financial advisors who specialize in dividend growth investing or portfolio management. Their expertise can help you make informed decisions and navigate complex financial situations.

In the ever-changing financial landscape, adaptation, innovation, and staying ahead are essential for dividend growth investors. By remaining flexible in your approach, exploring emerging opportunities, and staying informed, you can continue to thrive in dynamic markets and work toward your financial goals. As you embark on this journey, remember that dividend growth investing is not only about the destination but also about the strategies and experiences that shape your financial future.

Chapter 13: Conclusion

As you near the culmination of your journey in dividend growth investing and approach the threshold of financial independence and retirement, it's an opportune moment to reflect on the path you've traversed. This chapter explores the timeless joys inherent in dividend growth investing, the fulfillment of achieving financial independence, and embracing retirement with grace.

Reflecting on the Journey

1. **The Seeds of Financial Freedom:** Reflect upon the initial steps you took in your dividend growth journey. Perhaps it started with a single stock purchase or a commitment to consistent saving and investing. Acknowledge the progress you've made since those early days.

2. **Lessons from Setbacks:** Recall the challenges and setbacks you encountered along the way. Each obstacle provided an opportunity to learn and adapt your strategy. Resilience in the face of adversity has been a hallmark of your journey.

3. **The Power of Patience:** Consider how patience has been a constant companion. Dividend growth investing requires unwavering patience to allow the magic of compounding to work its wonders. Reflect on how your long-term perspective has served you well.

The Timeless Joys of Dividend Growth Investing

1. **A Stream of Income:** The timeless joy of dividend growth investing lies in the steady stream of income it provides. Whether you're in the midst of your career or enjoying retirement, the dividends you receive offer financial stability and flexibility.

2. **Peace of Mind:** Knowing that your investments generate income even in turbulent market conditions provides peace of mind. This security allows you to navigate life's uncertainties with confidence.

3. **The Beauty of Compounding:** Reflect on the beauty of compounding returns. Over time, reinvested dividends have multiplied your investment principal, allowing your portfolio to grow exponentially.

Embracing Financial Independence and Retirement with Grace

1. **Financial Independence:** Achieving financial independence is a profound accomplishment. It liberates you from financial constraints and offers the freedom to live life on your terms. Embrace this independence with gratitude and humility.

2. **The Freedom to Choose:** Retirement is not just an end but a new beginning. It grants you the freedom to choose how you spend your time, whether pursuing passions, exploring the world, or dedicating yourself to causes you care about.

3. **Legacy and Philanthropy:** Consider your desires for legacy planning and philanthropy. Retirement can be an ideal time to leave a financial legacy for your heirs or make a lasting impact on the world through charitable endeavors.

4. **The Art of Giving Back:** Embracing retirement with grace often involves giving back to your community or contributing to causes that matter to you. Volunteering your time, expertise, or resources can be profoundly rewarding.

5. **Staying Engaged:** Retirement is not about idleness but about staying engaged in life. Embrace opportunities for personal growth, continued learning, and pursuing new experiences.

6. **Passing Down Wisdom:** Share the wisdom you've gained on your financial journey with younger generations. Your experiences and insights can empower them to make informed financial decisions.

7. **Contentment:** Ultimately, retirement is about finding contentment in the life you've created. Embrace the simple joys of everyday living, spending time with loved ones, and savoring the fruits of your labor.

The journey of dividend growth investing is a testament to your dedication, discipline, and long-term perspective. As you reflect on this journey and approach the threshold of retirement, savor the timeless joys it has brought you. Embrace financial independence and retirement with grace, knowing that the path you've chosen has led to a future filled with possibilities, fulfillment, and the opportunity to make a meaningful impact on your own life and the lives of others.

Appendix A: Glossary of Key Terms

1. **Dividend:** A payment made by a corporation to its shareholders, usually in the form of cash or additional shares of stock, as a portion of its earnings.

2. **Dividend Yield:** The annual dividend income earned as a percentage of the investment's current market price. It's calculated by dividing the annual dividend per share by the stock's current market price.

3. **Dividend Aristocrats:** A group of S&P 500 companies with a track record of consistently increasing their dividends for at least 25 consecutive years.

4. **Payout Ratio:** The percentage of a company's earnings that is paid out to shareholders in the form of dividends. It's calculated by dividing dividends per share by earnings per share.

5. **Ex-Dividend Date:** The date on or after which a buyer of a stock will not receive the next dividend payment. Investors need to purchase the stock before the ex-dividend date to be eligible for the upcoming dividend.

6. **Dividend Reinvestment Plan (DRIP):** A program that allows shareholders to automatically reinvest their dividend income by purchasing additional shares of the same stock, often at a discount.

7. **Record Date:** The date on which a company determines the list of shareholders eligible to receive dividends. Shareholders on record as of this date will receive the dividend.

8. **Pay Date:** The date on which dividend payments are actually distributed to eligible shareholders.

9. **Blue-Chip Stocks:** Large, well-established, and financially stable companies known for their history of reliable dividends and overall stability.

10. **Stock Dividend:** A dividend paid in the form of additional shares of stock rather than cash. It doesn't change the total value of the investment but increases the number of shares held.

11. **Cumulative Preferred Stock:** A type of preferred stock that accumulates unpaid dividends and pays them to shareholders in the future if the company is unable to make dividend payments in a given period.

12. **Declaration Date:** The date on which a company's board of directors announces its intention to pay a dividend. It includes the dividend amount and payment date.

13. **Special Dividend:** An extra dividend payment made by a company, typically as a result of extraordinary profits, asset sales, or other one-time events.

14. **Qualified Dividend:** A dividend that is eligible for favorable tax treatment in many countries, typically subject to lower tax rates than ordinary income.

15. **Non-Qualified Dividend:** A dividend that doesn't meet the criteria for favorable tax treatment and is generally taxed as ordinary income.

16. **Total Return:** The combined return from both capital appreciation (changes in stock price) and dividend income from an investment.

These terms provide a foundation for understanding dividend investing, but the world of investing can be complex. If you're considering dividend investing, it's important to further explore these concepts and seek professional advice to make informed investment decisions.

Appendix B: Sample Dividend Portfolio

Here's a brief sample dividend stock portfolio. This diversified portfolio consists of well-established companies from various sectors, offering a mix of income and potential for dividend growth. Please note that this is a simplified example and not personalized investment advice. It's important to conduct your own research and consider your financial goals and risk tolerance before making investment decisions.

1. Apple Inc. (AAPL):

- Dividend Yield (as of September 2023): Approximately 0.6%

- Apple is a technology leader known for its iconic products and has a history of dividend growth.

2. Microsoft Corporation (MSFT):

- Dividend Yield (as of September 2023): Approximately 0.9%

- Microsoft is a technology giant offering software, cloud services, and more. It has consistently increased its dividends.

3. Johnson & Johnson (JNJ):

- Dividend Yield (as of September 2023): Approximately 3%

- Johnson & Johnson is a diversified healthcare company with a strong commitment to dividend payments.

4. Procter & Gamble Co. (PG):

- Dividend Yield (as of September 2023): Approximately 2.5%

- Procter & Gamble is a consumer goods conglomerate known for household brands and dividend reliability.

5. PepsiCo, Inc. (PEP):

- Dividend Yield (as of September 2023): Approximately 3%

- PepsiCo is a global leader in beverages and snacks, with a history of consistent dividend payments.

6. The Home Depot, Inc. (HD):

- Dividend Yield (as of September 2023): Approximately 2.7%

- Home Depot is a leading home improvement retailer known for its stability and shareholder-friendly policies.

7. Visa Inc. (V):

- Dividend Yield (as of September 2023): Approximately 0.8%

- Visa operates in the financial services sector and participates in the growth of electronic payments.

8. 3M Company (MMM):

- Dividend Yield (as of September 2023): Approximately 6.5%

- 3M is a diversified industrial conglomerate with a history of dividend increases.

9. NextEra Energy, Inc. (NEE):

- Dividend Yield (as of September 2023): Approximately 3.2%

- NextEra Energy is a leading renewable energy company, offering both income and sustainable growth potential.

10. Realty Income Corp. (O):

- Dividend Yield (as of September 2023): Approximately 6.1%

- Realty Income, often referred to as "The Monthly Dividend Company," specializes in real estate investment and offers regular monthly dividend payments.

This diversified portfolio includes companies from various sectors, including technology, healthcare, consumer goods, retail, finance, industrial, energy, and real estate. It provides a mix of dividend yield and potential for dividend growth, catering to income-focused investors with different risk tolerances. Remember to conduct thorough research and consider your unique financial situation when building your investment portfolio.

Appendix C: Recommended Reading List

To gain a comprehensive understanding of dividend investing and retirement planning, consider reading the following recommended books:

Books on Dividend Investing:

1. **"The Single Best Investment: Creating Wealth with Dividend Growth" by Lowell Miller:** This book explores the concept of investing in dividend-paying stocks and their potential to provide consistent income and wealth creation.

2. **"The Dividend Mantra Way" by Jason Fieber:** Written by a dividend growth investor, this book offers insights into building a dividend-focused portfolio, emphasizing the importance of patience and discipline.

3. **"The Ultimate Dividend Playbook: Income, Insight, and Independence for Today's Investor" by Josh Peters:** Josh Peters, an expert on dividend investing, provides practical guidance on selecting and managing dividend-paying stocks.

4. **"Dividends Still Don't Lie: The Truth About Investing in Blue Chip Stocks and Winning in the Stock Market" by Kelley Wright:** This book offers a value-based approach to dividend investing, focusing on the analysis of dividend yield and price.

5. **"Dividend Growth Machine: How to Build a Worry-Free Retirement with Dividend Stocks" by Nathan Winklepleck:** This book discusses strategies for creating a retirement income stream through dividend growth investing.

Books on Retirement Planning:

1. **"The Total Money Makeover: A Proven Plan for Financial Fitness" by Dave Ramsey:** While not solely focused on retirement, this book provides practical advice on achieving financial independence and securing your retirement.

2. **"How to Make Your Money Last: The Indispensable Retirement Guide" by Jane Bryant Quinn:** This comprehensive guide covers various aspects of retirement planning, including managing investments, Social Security, and healthcare.

3. **"The Bogleheads' Guide to Retirement Planning" by Taylor Larimore, Mel Lindauer, and Richard A. Ferri:** Based on the principles of John Bogle, this book offers a step-by-step guide to planning for a financially secure retirement.

4. **"The New Retirementality: Planning Your Life and Living Your Dreams...at Any Age You Want" by Mitch Anthony:** This book challenges traditional notions of retirement and encourages readers to consider a more fulfilling and flexible approach to their post-career years.

5. **"Retire Before Mom and Dad: The Simple Numbers Behind a Lifetime of Financial Freedom" by Rob Berger:** Focused on achieving early retirement, this book provides strategies for saving, investing, and building wealth to retire on your terms.

6. **"Your Money or Your Life: 9 Steps to Transforming Your Relationship with Money and Achieving Financial Independence" by Vicki Robin and Joe Dominguez:** This classic book offers a holistic approach to financial independence and early retirement, emphasizing mindful spending and investing.

These books cover a range of topics related to dividend investing and retirement planning, from the basics of building a dividend portfolio to the broader aspects of achieving financial independence and securing a comfortable retirement. Reading multiple books can provide a well-rounded perspective and help you tailor your financial strategies to your specific goals and circumstances.